BOSTON TERRIER HISTORY

The gentle and affectionate Boston Terrier was originally envisioned as a small fighting dog and was developed in much the same way as the other fighting breeds of the 19th century — by crossing formidable bulldogs with a variety of tough and tenacious and stamina, so the most compact bulldogs were used for breeding.

During the 1850s, the bulldog and terrier cross became quite popular and dogs resulting from such breedings were called Bull-and-Terriers or Half-and-Halfs. Eventually these Half-and-Halfs

The Boston Terrier is distinguished as the first dog breed to be "made in America," and also as the first native dog breed to be recognized by the American Kennel Club.

terriers. The 19th century Bulldog looked quite different than our modern sourmug. He was taller, leaner and more agile, with straight front legs and a longer muzzle. In creating the Boston Terrier, the accent was on smallness in addition to strength were bred to each other, and the ancient Bull-and-Terrier became the ancestor of the modern Boston Terrier, as well as the Staffordshire Bull Terrier, American Staffordshire Terrier, Bull Terrier and American Pit Bull Terrier.

Sturdy and compact, the Boston Terrier was originally bred to be a small fighting dog.

Distinguished as the first dog breed to be "made in America," and the first native dog breed to gain American Kennel Club recognition, the history of the Boston Terrier began in the Beacon Hill section of Boston, Massachusetts, around 1870. That's when William O'Brien sold a dog named "Judge" to Robert C. Hooper, who recorded the dog's name as Hooper's Judge. Destined to become the ancestor of almost every modern-day Boston Terrier, Hooper's Judge had been imported from Europe and was the result of a cross between an English Bulldog and one of the various English terriers. He was 32 pounds of solid muscle; a dark brindle with a white stripe up his wide, blocky face.

Most dog breeds can't be traced all the way back to the individual dogs that influenced their earliest development, but the Boston Terrier can. The Bull-and-Terrier named Hooper's Judge was bred to a solidly built, 20-pound white female owned by Edward Burnett of Southboro, Massachusetts. Her name appears on some records as Burnett's Gyp and on others as Burnett's Kate. It's probably safe to assume that Kate is correct because the word "gyp" was occasionally used in place of the word "bitch" to refer to a female dog.

Descendants of Judge and Kate included Well's Eph, a short and strongly built dark-brindle dog with even, white markings. A

During the 1850s, Bulldog and terrier crosses were very popular. These half-and-halfs went on to become the ancestors of today's modern Boston Terrier.

breeding between Eph and a solid, 20-pound, golden-brindle female named Tobin's Kate produced Barnard's Tom. Tom weighed 23 pounds and had a dark brindle coat, white markings and a short screw tail. When bred to Kelly's Nell, a muscular 20-pounder with an unevenly marked half-brindle and half-white face, Tom sired Barnard's Mike. Many breed historians believe Mike was the breed's most influential ancestor in terms of establishing the breed's unique appearance. He was a 25-pound dark brindle with a white blaze, white chest and white feet. His body was short and blocky and he had large eyes and a screw tail.

During the early years, there was much inbreeding to set breed type. Occasional outcrosses were also made, sometimes to French Bulldogs, but most often to selected small terriers. Size gradually diminished, but spirit and intelligence did not. While the new breed never became the miniature fighting dog originally intended, it quickly developed a loyal following. Highly trainable and compact, yet able to handle itself if threatened, the new breed soon became a popular pet.

In 1889, about 30 owners of the new breed from in and around Boston got together to form a dog club. They called their group the American Bull Terrier Club, and their dogs Bull Terriers or Round Heads. This angered the Bull Terrier breeders, who said the new breed was totally different

During the early years, breeders gradually diminished size, but the breed's spirit and intelligence remained, and the Boston soon became a popular pet.

than their established breed and should not have a name that was practically the same. To keep the peace, the American Bull Terrier Club changed its name to the Boston Terrier Club of America in 1891, and by 1893 the American Kennel Club recognized both the new breed and the fledgling club.

Boston Terrier breeders seemed to have an affinity for the show ring right from the start, and competing to have the best-looking Boston prompted them to breed the best to the best until their dogs were standardized in appearance and bred true to type. During the 1920s, the breed was so popular that 30 percent of the dogs entered in some shows were

The Boston Terrier has been widely acclaimed for his good looks and excellent disposition.

Fanciers originally called their club the American Bull Terrier Club but changed the name to the Boston Terrier Club of America in 1891.

Boston Terriers. By the 1930s, the breed was such a runaway best-seller that people who wanted to make quick money got into the act, breeding inferior dogs at a fast pace. The unfortunate buyers who purchased these sad specimens didn't want another, so the Boston Terrier declined in popularity during the 1940s. Soon the "quick-buck breeders" abandoned the breed, leaving the ethical breeders to repair the damage. These conscientious fanciers soon produced sturdy and stable Boston Terriers again. Eventually the breed's popularity leveled off and its quality remained high. In 1996, the Boston Terrier ranked 23rd in popularity out of the 140 breeds recognized by the American Kennel Club, and he has been widely acclaimed for decades for his good looks and excellent disposition.

This Boston, owned by W. Verhaegen, has the large, expressive eyes for which the breed is known.

CHARACTERISTICS OF THE BOSTON TERRIER

Lively and friendly, the Boston Terrier is a highly intelligent, smallish dog with a short, shiny coat, an equally short muzzle and large, expressive eyes. Although his ancestors were bred to fight other dogs, the Boston Terrier never achieved fame for its fighting prowess. Instead, he came to be loved for the many endearing qualities that make him a priceless pet. Right from the start he behaved like a jaunty gentleman, providing first-class companionship to his human owners. A smaller dog today than his ancestors were, the Boston Terrier is still one of the biggest breeds of all when it comes to intelligence, loyalty, zest for life and a capacity for fun.

Handsome, sensitive and affectionate, the Boston Terrier is classified by the American Kennel Club as a Non-Sporting breed — another word for companion dog.

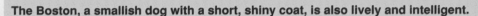

The Boston, a smallish dog with a short, shiny coat, is also lively and intelligent.

Cherished for his endearing qualities, the Boston rewards his family with first-class companionship.

apartment or on a spacious farm. The short and shiny Boston Terrier coat needs little grooming to stay glossy and clean. If you would rather spend your time petting and playing instead of grooming, this animated, tuxedo-clad dog could be the right breed for you. But if you love the look and feel of fluffy or curly-coated dogs, and look forward to brushing and fussing, you may find a longer-coated breed more fulfilling.

The Boston Terrier is first and foremost a companion and house dog. Unable to tolerate cold temperatures or drafty basements, he needs cozy quarters near his human family and can get enough exercise even in a small apartment. When

And that's exactly what he has been for over a hundred years.

Highly adaptable, a Boston Terrier can be happy in a small

Whether playing or resting, the highly adaptable Boston is happy in a small apartment or on a spacious estate.

When given the opportunity the Boston is always raring to go.

allowed outdoors, he should be in a securely fenced yard with sufficient shade, shelter and fresh water. When taken for a walk he should always be on lead. A physically fit Boston will be delighted to accompany his owner on long walks in pleasant weather, but will prefer his cozy bed on rainy evenings and frosty mornings. However, Bostons can be exercised outside during the winter, and usually learn to "go potty" on lead very quickly in order to return to the comfort of indoor heating. Owners who exercise their Bostons by turning them loose in fenced yards should be careful not to leave their dogs outside long enough to chill them. Bitter cold and bare bellies are not a good match.

The typical Boston adores children, and will happily play games with them for hours provided the youngsters have been taught how to safely and gently handle a pet. Young children should enjoy their Boston with adult supervision until they are old enough to realize that dogs have intelligence and feelings, and are not battery operated toys fit for pulling and poking. Special care must be taken to keep toddlers from injuring a Boston's big eyes.

Most Boston Terriers are alert watchdogs, barking sharply when a stranger approaches the door. Perceptive pets who take their cues from their owners' reactions, they will soon welcome the stranger with kisses, if a family

Though a small breed, the Boston can find his way into big trouble in a hurry.

member seems sincerely glad to see the person. Because they are so responsive to gentle, consistent training, many Bostons excel at competitive activities such as obedience and agility, or rewarding avocations such as therapy work. In fact, many Bostons can barely contain their glee when taking center stage. But the Boston's quick intelligence is that never stops thinking — can turn a neglected or untrained Boston into a wily rogue. Don't get a dog at all if you don't have time to give him the vital gift of basic training. Dogs are social animals and need guidance and companionship. There are many other types of pets available that readily adapt to long hours of solitude.

All puppies are irresistible, and Bostons are certainly no exception. Make sure the Boston will fit into your home and lifestyle before making the commitment to own one.

not a plus in every situation. It can be a problem for owners who don't take the time to train their pet.

Just because this breed is relatively small doesn't mean it won't find its way into trouble when left to its own devices. The same qualities that make the breed so charming — spirit, energy, love of games and a brain

Socialization brings out the best in a Boston's personality. It means familiarizing a puppy (or new dog) with the people, animals, objects and noises he may encounter during everyday life. Vaccinated puppies should be introduced to friendly people of all ages and both sexes, and to non-menacing, well-mannered dogs. They should ride in cars other than for trips to the veterinarian; walk on varied footing, such as linoleum, concrete, grass, wood and carpet; and encounter bicycles, shopping carts, joggers, people in wheelchairs and traffic sounds — all while on lead, of course. Always be cautious for your little dog, as many Boston

in the mood for a romp. In general, Bostons get along well with other pets, even cats, but an occasional male may be scrappy with other male dogs.

When learning tricks at home, or when attending obedience or agility classes, Boston Terriers are happy and willing workers. Since

Always in the mood for a romp, some Boston pups need to be reminded of their status

Terriers don't seem to recognize that they are small. Bostons have been known to approach even gigantic dogs and use canine body language, such as play-bowing, to invite them to play. While most dogs recognize the Boston's good will instantly and eagerly join in the fun, not every big dog will be

they are inclined to be obedient, and are extremely receptive to praise, training them is just a matter of a little time and patience. Some Bostons have a slight stubborn streak, but a composed and consistent owner will easily win out and the dog will soon perform as if obeying

Despite his playful nature, the Boston readily adapts to a more sedate household.

commands was his idea all along. Training your Boston Terrier is more than worth the effort, because once a Boston learns the rules, or perfects a trick, he never forgets.

The Boston Terrier loves human companionship and will contentedly curl up in a loving lap, emitting an amusing variety of grunts, snorts and wheezes while thumping his tiny tail. Anxious to please, he usually adjusts to his owner's activity level. This is a plus if you are moderately active, but if you seldom exercise, your inactive Boston may become dangerously overweight. Prevent this by tossing balls for your Boston to chase and cheering him on as he play-kills his favorite toy. Curious and comical, with a well-developed sense of fun, your Boston will play at the slightest

provocation. The breed retains its puppyish love of toys and games into old age, so enticing a Boston to exercise is always easy. While the breed prefers an active lifestyle, it easily adapts to a more sedate household, especially if acquired young. In fact, Boston Terriers are the beloved pets of thousands of senior citizens.

Living with a Boston Terrier is never boring. Extremely fun-loving, this dog greets each day with renewed cheer. A happy, healthy Boston moves with ease and grace and seldom goes anywhere at a walk that can be reached at a trot. He loves his family and enjoys his toys, and whether his owner chooses to join in the games or simply watch, the spectacle is entertaining.

Chewing on a Gumabone® will be one of your Boston Terrier's favorite things to do.

STANDARD OF THE BOSTON TERRIER

General Appearance—The Boston Terrier is a lively, highly intelligent, smooth coated, short-headed, compactly built, short-tailed, well balanced dog, brindle, seal or black in color and evenly marked with white. The head is in proportion to the size of the dog and the expression indicates a high degree of intelligence.

The body is rather short and well knit, the limbs strong and neatly turned, the tail is short and no feature is so prominent that the dog appears badly proportioned. The dog conveys an impression of determination, strength and activity, with style of a high order; carriage easy and graceful. A proportionate

The Boston conveys strength, determination and action, while maintaining his style and grace.

The Boston Terrier's head is in proportion to the size of the dog and the expression indicates a high degree of intelligence.

The length of the legs must balance the length of the body to give the Boston its strikingly square appearance.

combination of "Color and White Markings" is a particularly distinctive feature of a representative specimen.

"Balance, Expression, Color and White Markings"should be given particular consideration in determining the relative value of GENERAL APPEARANCE to other points.

Size, Proportion, Substance—Weight is divided by classes as follows: Under 15 pounds; 15 pounds and under 20 pounds; 20 pounds and not to exceed 25 pounds. The length of leg must balance with the length of body to give the Boston Terrier its striking square appearance. The Boston Terrier is a sturdy dog and must not appear to be either spindly or coarse. The bone and muscle must be in proportion as well as an enhancement to the dog's weight and structure.

Fault: Blocky or chunky in appearance.

Influence of Sex. In a comparison of specimens of each sex, the only evident difference is a slight refinement in the bitch's conformation.

Head—The *skull* is square, flat on top, free from wrinkles, cheeks flat, brow abrupt and the stop well defined. The ideal Boston Terrier *expression* is alert and kind, indicating a high degree of intelligence. This is a most important characteristic of the breed. The *eyes* are wide apart, large and round and dark in color. The eyes are set square in the skull and the outside corners wrinkles, shorter in length than in width or depth; not exceeding in length approximately one-third of the length of the skull. The muzzle from stop to end of the nose is parallel to the top of the skull.

The *nose* is black and wide, with a well defined line between the nostrils. Disqualify: Dudley nose.

The *jaw* is broad and square with short regular teeth. The bite is even or sufficiently undershot

The Boston's muzzle is short, square, wide and deep, and in proportion to the skull.

are on a line with the cheeks as viewed from the front. **Disqualify:** Eyes blue in color or any trace of blue. The **ears** are small, carried erect, either natural or cropped to conform to the shape of the head and situated as near to the corners of the skull as possible.

The *muzzle* is short, square, wide and deep and in proportion to the skull. It is free from to square the muzzle. The chops are of good depth, but not pendulous, completely covering the teeth when the mouth is closed. **Serious Fault:** Wry mouth.

Head Faults: Eyes showing too much white or haw. Pinched or wide nostrils. Size of ears out of proportion to the size of the head. **Serious Head Faults:** Any

The Boston's chest is deep with good width and well-sprung ribs.

showing of the tongue or teeth when the mouth is closed.

Neck, Topline and Body—The length of **neck** must display an image of balance to the total dog. It is slightly arched, carrying the head gracefully and setting neatly into the shoulders. The **back** is just short enough to square the body. The **topline** is level and the rump curves slightly to the set-on of the tail. The **chest** is deep with good width, ribs well sprung and carried well back to the loins. The body should appear short. The **tail** is set on low, short, fine and tapering, straight or screw and must not be carried above the horizontal. (Note: The preferred tail does not exceed in length more than one-quarter the distance from set-on to hock.) **Disqualify:** Docked tail. **Body Faults:** Gaily carried tail. **Serious Body Faults:** Roach back, sway back, slab-sided.

Forequarters—The **shoulders** are sloping and well laid back, which allows for the Boston

Terrier's stylish movement. The **elbows** stand neither in nor out. The **forelegs** are set moderately wide apart and on a line with the upper tip of the shoulder blades. The forelegs are straight in bone with short, strong pasterns. The dewclaws may be removed. The **feet** are small, round and compact, turned neither in nor out, with well arched toes and short nails. **Faults:** Legs lacking in substance; splay feet.

Hindquarters—The **thighs** are strong and well muscled, bent at the stifles and set true. The **hocks** are short to the feet, turning neither in nor out, with a well defined hock joint. The **feet** are small and compact with short nails. **Fault:** Straight in stifle.

Gait—The gait of the Boston Terrier is that of a sure footed, straight gaited dog, forelegs and hind legs moving straight ahead in line with perfect rhythm, each step indicating grace and power.

The gait of the Boston is sure-footed and straight; with his legs moving in line with perfect rhythm.

Required markings called for in the standard include a white muzzle band, a white blaze between the eyes and a white forechest.

Gait Faults: There will be no rolling, paddling, or weaving, when gaited. Hackney gait. *Serious Gait Faults:* Any crossing movement, either front or rear.

Coat—The coat is short, smooth, bright and fine in texture.

Color and Markings—Brindle, seal, or black with white markings. Brindle is preferred ONLY if all other qualities are equal. (Note: SEAL DEFINED. Seal appears black except it has a red cast when viewed in the sun or bright light. *Disqualify:* Solid black, solid brindle or solid seal without required white markings. Gray or liver colors.

Required Markings: White muzzle band, white blaze between the eyes, white forechest.

Desired Markings: White muzzle band, even white blaze between the eyes and over the head, white collar, white forechest, white on part or whole of forelegs and hind legs below the hocks. (Note: A representative specimen should not be penalized for not possessing "Desired Markings.")

A dog with a preponderance of white on the head or body must possess sufficient merit otherwise to counteract its deficiencies.

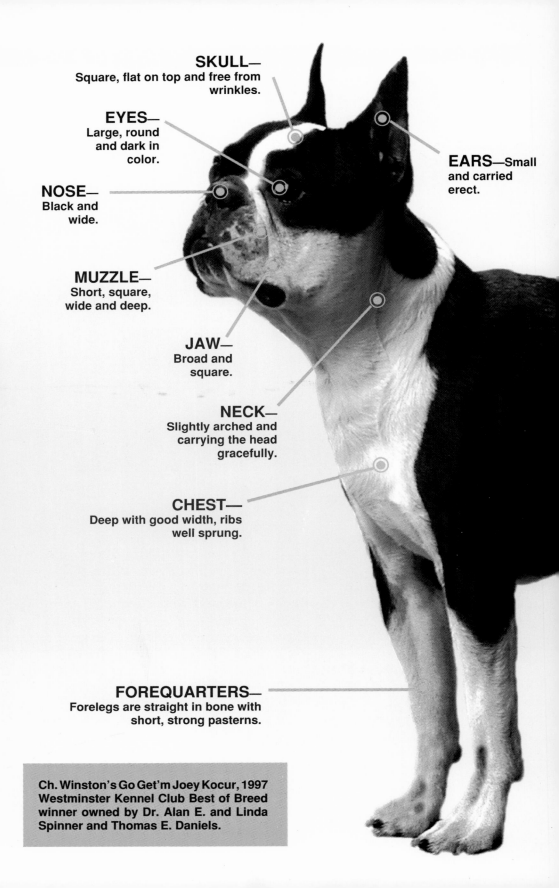

SKULL—
Square, flat on top and free from wrinkles.

EYES—
Large, round and dark in color.

EARS—Small and carried erect.

NOSE—
Black and wide.

MUZZLE—
Short, square, wide and deep.

JAW—
Broad and square.

NECK—
Slightly arched and carrying the head gracefully.

CHEST—
Deep with good width, ribs well sprung.

FOREQUARTERS—
Forelegs are straight in bone with short, strong pasterns.

Ch. Winston's Go Get'm Joey Kocur, 1997 Westminster Kennel Club Best of Breed winner owned by Dr. Alan E. and Linda Spinner and Thomas E. Daniels.

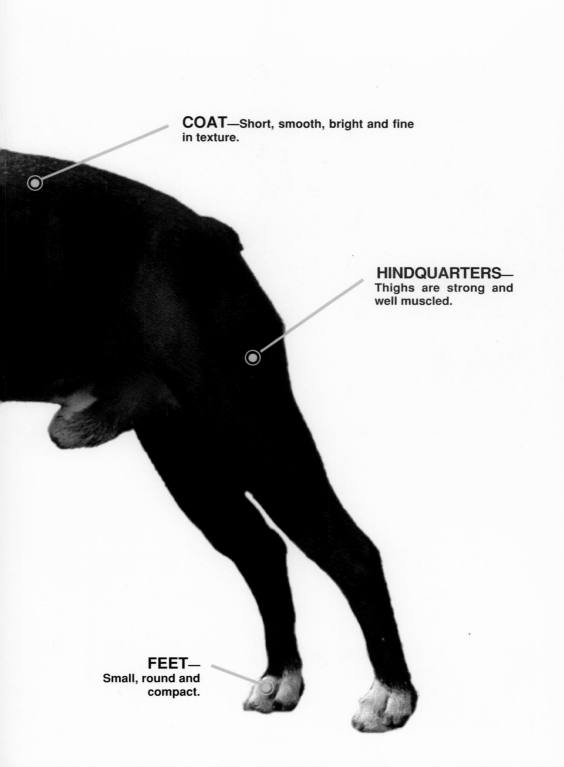

COAT—Short, smooth, bright and fine in texture.

HINDQUARTERS— Thighs are strong and well muscled.

FEET— Small, round and compact.

The short-smooth coat of the Boston is no match for bad weather. Don't allow your Boston to get chilled during the colder months.

Temperament—The Boston Terrier is a friendly and lively dog. The breed has an excellent disposition and a high degree of intelligence, which makes the Boston Terrier an incomparable companion.

Summary—The clean-cut short backed body of the Boston Terrier coupled with the unique characteristics of his square head and jaw, and his striking markings have resulted in a most dapper and charming American original: The Boston Terrier.

DISQUALIFICATIONS
Eyes blue in color or any trace of blue.
Dudley nose.
Docked tail.
Solid black, solid brindle, or solid seal without required white markings.
Gray or liver colors.
Approved January 9, 1990
Effective February 28, 1990

FEEDING YOUR BOSTON TERRIER

Now let's talk about feeding your Boston Terrier, a subject so simple that it's amazing there is so much nonsense and misunderstanding about it. Is it expensive to feed a Boston Terrier? No, it is not! You can feed dogs flatly refuse to eat nice, fresh beef. They pick around it and eat everything else. But meat—bah! Why? They aren't accustomed to it! They'd eat rabbit fast enough, but they refuse beef because they aren't used to it.

It is best to feed your new Boston puppy the same food he was eating before you brought him home. Any change in food should be made gradually.

your Boston Terrier economically and keep him in perfect shape the year round, or you can feed him expensively. He'll thrive either way, and let's see why this is true.

First of all, remember a Boston Terrier is a dog. Dogs do not have a high degree of selectivity in their food, and unless you spoil them with great variety (and possibly turn them into poor, "picky" eaters) they will eat almost anything that they become accustomed to. Many

VARIETY NOT NECESSARY

A good general rule of thumb is forget all human preferences and don't give a thought to variety. Choose the right diet for your Boston Terrier and feed it to him day after day, year after year, winter and summer. But what is the right diet?

Hundreds of thousands of dollars have been spent in canine nutrition research. The results are pretty conclusive, so you needn't go into a lot of experimenting with trials of this and that every other week. Research has proven just what your dog needs to eat and to keep healthy.

satisfactory, and easily available in stores everywhere in containers of five to 50 pounds. Larger amounts cost less per pound, usually.

Bostons are usually not very selective eaters, unless you make them so. Feed your Boston what is good for him and forget about human dietary preference.

DOG FOOD

There are almost as many right diets as there are dog experts, but the basic diet most often recommended is one that consists of a dry food, either meal or kibble form. There are several of excellent quality, manufactured by reliable companies, research tested, and nationally advertised. They are inexpensive, highly

If you have a choice of brands, it is usually safer to choose the better known one; but even so, carefully read the analysis on the package. Do not choose any food in which the protein level is less than 25 percent, and be sure that this protein comes from both animal and vegetable sources. The good dog foods have meat meal, fish meal, liver, and such, plus protein from alfalfa and soy beans, as well as some dried-milk product. Note the vitamin content carefully. See that they are all there in good proportions; and be especially certain that the food contains properly high levels of vitamins A and D, two of the most perishable and important ones. Note the B-complex level, but don't worry about carbohydrate and mineral levels. These substances are plentiful and cheap and not likely to be lacking in a good brand.

Several small meals a day is not only better for your Boston but essential for deep-chested dogs.

The advice given for how to choose a dry food also applies to moist or canned types of dog foods, if you decide to feed one of these.

Having chosen a really good food, feed it to your Boston Terrier as the manufacturer directs. And once you've started, stick to it. Never change if you can possibly help it. A switch from one meal or kibble-type food can usually be made without too much upset; however, a change will almost invariably give you (and your Boston Terrier) some trouble.

WHEN SUPPLEMENTS ARE NEEDED

Now what about supplements of various kinds, minerals and vitamins, or the various oils? They are all okay to add to your Boston Terrier's food. However, if you are feeding your Boston Terrier a correct diet, and this is easy to do, no supplements are necessary unless your Boston Terrier has been improperly fed, has been sick, or is having puppies. Vitamins and minerals are naturally present in all the foods; and to ensure against any loss through processing, they are added in concentrated form to the dog food you use. Except on the advice of your veterinarian, added amounts of vitamins can prove harmful to your Boston Terrier! The same risk goes with minerals.

FEEDING SCHEDULE

When and how much food to give your Boston Terrier? Most dogs do better if fed two or three smaller meals per day—this is not only better but vital to larger and deep-chested dogs. As to how to prepare the food and how much to give, it is generally best to follow the directions on the food package. Your own Boston Terrier may want a little more or a little less.

Fresh, cool water should always be available to your Boston Terrier. This is important to good health throughout his lifetime.

Carrots are rich in fiber,carbohydrates and vitamin A. The Carrot Bone™ by Nylabone®
is a durable chew containing no plastics or artificial ingredients and can be served as-is,
in a bone-hard form, or microwaved to a biscuit consistency.

ALL BOSTON TERRIERS NEED TO CHEW

Puppies and young Boston Terriers need something with resistance to chew on while their teeth and jaws are developing—for cutting the puppy teeth, to induce growth of the permanent teeth under the puppy teeth, to assist in getting rid of the puppy teeth at the proper time, to help the permanent teeth through the gums, to ensure normal jaw development, and to settle the permanent teeth solidly in the jaws.

The adult Boston Terrier's desire to chew stems from the instinct for tooth cleaning, gum massage, and jaw exercise—plus the need for an outlet for periodic doggie tensions.

This is why dogs, especially puppies and young dogs, will often destroy property worth hundreds of dollars when their chewing instinct is not diverted from their owner's possessions. And this is why you should provide your Boston Terrier with something to chew—something that has the necessary functional qualities, is desirable from the Boston Terrier's viewpoint, and is safe for him.

It is very important that your Boston Terrier not be permitted to chew on anything he can break or on any indigestible thing from which he can bite sizable chunks. Sharp pieces, such as from a bone which can be broken by a dog, may pierce the intestinal wall and kill. Indigestible things that can be bitten off in chunks, such as from shoes or rubber or plastic toys, may cause an intestinal stoppage (if not regurgitated) and bring painful death, unless surgery is promptly performed.

Strong natural bones, such as 4-to 8-inch lengths of round shin bone from mature beef—either the kind you can get from a butcher or one of the variety available commercially in pet stores—may serve your Boston Terrier's teething needs if his mouth is large enough to handle them effectively. You may be tempted to give your Boston Terrier puppy a smaller bone and he may not be able to break it when you do, but puppies grow rapidly and the power of their jaws constantly increases until maturity. This means that a growing Boston Terrier may break one of the smaller bones at any time, swallow the pieces, and die painfully before you realize what is wrong.

All hard natural bones are very abrasive. If your Boston Terrier is an avid chewer, natural bones may wear away his teeth prematurely; hence, they then should be taken away from your dog when the teething purposes have been served. The badly worn,

To help relieve doggie tension and to stimulate the gums for healthy teeth, furnish your adult Boston with something to chew on.

Your young Boston will need something to chew to help develop his teeth and jaws. The Nylabone® Rhino™ can entertain your pup while promoting oral health.

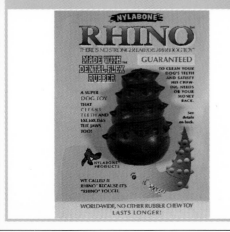

and usually painful, teeth of many mature dogs can be traced to excessive chewing on natural bones.

Contrary to popular belief, knuckle bones that can be chewed up and swallowed by your Boston Terrier provide little, if any, usable calcium or other nutriment. They do, however, disturb the digestion of most dogs and cause them to vomit the nourishing food they need.

Dried rawhide products of various types, shapes, sizes, and prices are available on the market and have become quite popular. However, they don't serve the primary chewing functions very well; they are a bit messy when wet from mouthing, and most Boston Terriers chew them up rather rapidly—but they have been considered safe for dogs until recently. Now, more and

To keep your Boston pup's chewing in check provide him with Nylabone ® product favorites such as the Nylafloss® nylon tug toy and the Gumabone® Frisbee™*. (The trademark Frisbee is used under license from Mattel, Inc. California, USA.)

more incidents of death, and near death, by strangulation have been reported to be the results of partially swallowed chunks of rawhide swelling in the throat. More recently, some veterinarians have been attributing cases of acute constipation to large pieces of incompletely digested rawhide in the intestine.

A new product, molded rawhide, is very safe. During the process, the rawhide is melted and then injection molded into the familiar dog shape. It is very hard and is eagerly accepted by

Roar-Hide™ is completely edible and is high in protein (over 86%) and low in fat (less than one-third of 1%). Unlike common rawhide, it is safer, less messy and more fun for your Boston.

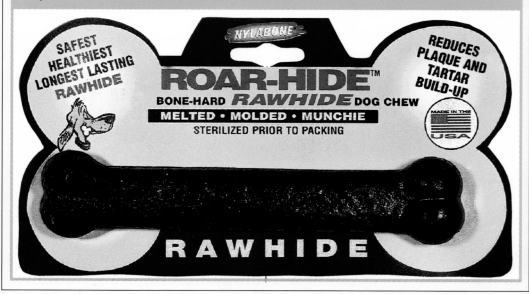

Boston Terriers. The melting process also sterilizes the rawhide. Don't confuse this with pressed rawhide, which is nothing more than small strips of rawhide squeezed together.

The nylon bones, especially those with natural meat and bone fractions added, are probably the most complete, safe, and economical answer to the chewing massage, much in the same way your toothbrush does it for you. The little projections are raked off and swallowed in the form of thin shavings, but the chemistry of the nylon is such that they break down in the stomach fluids and pass through without effect.

The toughness of the nylon provides the strong chewing resistance needed for important

If your Boston's need to chew is not properly diverted, he may find something of his own liking to chew on.

need. Dogs cannot break them or bite off sizable chunks; hence, they are completely safe—and being longer lasting than other things offered for the purpose, they are economical.

Hard chewing raises little bristle-like projections on the surface of the nylon bones—to provide effective interim tooth cleaning and vigorous gum jaw exercise and effectively aids teething functions, but there is no tooth wear because nylon is non-abrasive. Being inert, nylon does not support the growth of microorganisms; and it can be washed in soap and water or it can be sterilized by boiling or in an autoclave.

Nylabone® is highly recommended by veterinarians as

Keep your Boston on a regular feeding schedule or he may find his own supplements.

a safe, healthy nylon bone that can't splinter or chip. Nylabone® is frizzled by the dog's chewing action, creating a toothbrush-like surface that cleanses the teeth and massages the gums. Nylabone® is superior to the cheaper bones because it is made of virgin nylon, which is the strongest and longest-lasting type of nylon available. The cheaper bones are made from recycled or re-ground nylon scraps, and have a tendency to break apart and split easily.

Nothing, however, substitutes for periodic professional attention for your Boston Terrier's teeth and gums, not any more than your toothbrush can do that for you. Have your Boston Terrier's teeth cleaned at least once a year by your veterinarian (twice a year is better) and he will be happier, healthier, and far more pleasant to live with.

To keep your Boston healthy and his coat shiny, adhere to a proper diet and schedule.

GROOMING YOUR BOSTON TERRIER

A wash-and-wear breed, the Boston Terrier needs only a little grooming to absolutely glow. All you need to keep your Boston beautiful is a brush with short,

You can groom your Boston Terrier on your lap, but a grooming table may be easier on your back. Standing on a table also makes many dogs more

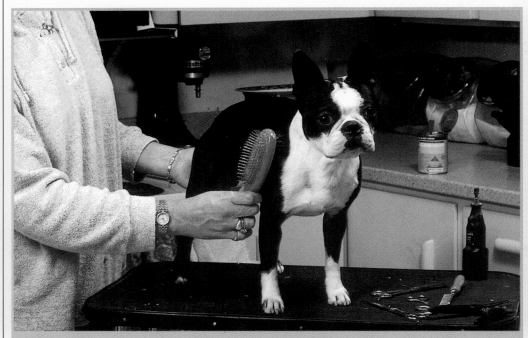

A few minutes of daily brushing with a natural bristle brush will maintain your Boston Terrier's naturally lustrous coat.

soft to medium bristles, or a hound glove (a mitten with natural bristles); a toe nail clipper; pH balanced dog shampoo (sometimes you may need insecticidal shampoo or dip); a soft toothbrush; and, perhaps, a grooming table. Additional bathing and grooming needs are probably already in your medicine chest.

cooperative. Grooming tables must be sturdy, have a non-slip surface such as ribbed rubber matting, and stand square, without a hint of wobble. You can make one yourself or buy one at a dog-show booth or through a pet supply catalog. They are available in a variety of sizes and the smallest is just right for most Boston Terriers. Grooming tables

Lonely without his mother or littermates, your Boston will look to you as his owner to be the leader of his pack.

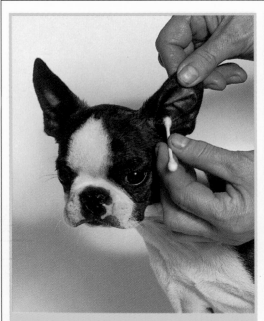

To clean your Boston's ears use a cotton swab dipped in peroxide or alcohol and gently swab the ridges—but don't go too deep!

COAT AND SKIN CARE

Just a minute or two of daily brushing with a natural bristle brush will keep your Boston Terrier's skin and coat healthy and shiny. Brushing removes dirt, dead hair, loose skin particles and dandruff while stimulating circulation and the secretion of natural skin oils.

While brushing your dog, check for ticks and fleas. Ticks are fairly easy to spot on a Boston Terrier's sleek coat, but they often hide between the toes, in the ears, in the slightly thicker hair of the neck and just in front of the tail. To find fleas, rough your dog's coat the opposite direction from the way it grows. Tiny black specks on the skin are a sign that fleas are present, even if you don't actually see a flea. Ask your

Grooming should be looked forward to by both dog and owner. It is time well spent as you bond with your Boston Terrier.

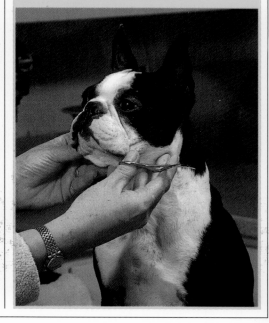

usually have folding legs so they are easy to move from one location to another or store when not in use. Some of them come with an adjustable arm and a loop that fits around the dog's neck to help keep him steady. Never leave your Boston alone on the table or even turn your back on him (even if the loop is around his neck). It takes less than an instant for a dog to jump or fall, and the results are often tragic.

Condition your Boston Terrier from puppyhood to accept grooming as a regular part of life, and he will soon enjoy your touch and look forward to the attention. Talk to him softly while you work, but if he becomes fidgety about being handled on any part of his body, say "NO" sharply and firmly and continue grooming.

veterinarian to recommend an insecticide shampoo or dip, and always use these products exactly as recommended on the label.

TOENAILS AND TEETH

Your Boston Terrier's toenails are too long if they touch the ground when he is standing still or make clicking noises on the floor when he walks. This is uncomfortable and can lead to splayed toes and an unattractive gait. Toenail trimmers made especially for dogs are available at most pet supply stores. They come in a variety of styles, and all of them work just fine.

To clip your Boston's nails, lift his foot up and forward. Then hold it firmly in your left hand so your right hand can do the trimming. (Reverse this if you are left-handed). When you cut the

Clip your Boston's nails regularly when he is a puppy so that he learns to be comfortable with the procedure.

To check your Boston Terrier's teeth for tartar, hold his head and gently push his lips upward.

nail properly, your dog will feel nothing more than slight pressure, the same as you feel when cutting your own toenails. But if you accidentally cut the quick, his nail will hurt and bleed and he may become leery of having his toenails trimmed. If your Boston Terrier has white nails, you can easily see the pink quick through each nail and avoid cutting it. Since you won't be able to see the quick if your Boston has dark nails, make the cut just outside the hooklike projection on the underside of the nail. Work under good lighting so you can cut your dog's nails without a mishap, but if you accidentally cut the quick, stop the bleeding with a styptic pencil made for human use, or use styptic powder sold at pet supply stores. Pressing the bleeding nail into a soft bar of soap for a minute or so will also stop the bleeding.

To check your Boston's teeth for tartar, hold his head steady and gently push his lips upward. If there are discolorations, use a soft baby toothbrush or the end of a damp washcloth dipped in baking soda.If the stains won't budge, check with your veterinarian. Your dog's teeth may need a professional cleaning.

BATHING

Your Boston Terrier will seldom need a bath if he is brushed briefly every day. Shampooing washes away the natural oils that moisturize the coat and skin, so bathe your dog only when necessary.

Equipment for a bath includes: old clothes (when your Boston shakes, you'll get wet); a tub, preferably with a drain so your dog won't have to stand in soapy water; a rubber mat for traction in the tub; a spray-nozzle hose attachment or an unbreakable cup for rinsing; pH balanced dog shampoo (or insecticide shampoo or dip if necessary); cotton balls; a washcloth; mineral oil; and a towel. Coat conditioner following the shampoo is optional. If you'd rather not bend over, bathe your Boston in the sink, but don't lose concentration for a second. If your slippery pet leaps to the floor, he could be severely injured.

Walk your Boston outside for a few minutes before beginning the bath. Otherwise he may want to rush outdoors to relieve himself

Use extra care when bathing your Boston in the sink to help avoid any accidents caused by slipping.

immediately following the bath, and he shouldn't go outside while still damp.

Start by placing part of a cotton ball inside each of your Boston's ears to keep the water out. Next, spray or pour warm water over your dog's body with the exception of his face and head. Put a few drops of shampoo on his back and massage the lather into his coat. (If you are using insecticide shampoo or dip, follow the label directions carefully.) Add a bit more shampoo as needed to clean his neck, legs, tail and underbelly. Take care to avoid getting soap in your dog's eyes, but if some suds accidentally splash into an eye, relieve the sting by placing a few drops of mineral oil in the inner corner of the eye. When your Boston Terrier

2-Brush™ by Nylabone® is made with two toothbrushes to clean both sides of your Boston's teeth at the same time. Each brush contains a reservoir to apply the toothpaste, which is specially formulated for dogs.

is clean, thoroughly rinse off the lather. Never rush this most important step. When shampoo dries in the coat it can cause intense itching and dull the shine.

Wipe your dog's face and head with a warm, well-wrung wash-cloth. Then remove the cotton from his ears and clean each ear gently with a dry cotton ball dipped in a tiny bit of mineral oil. Finish by wrapping your Boston Terrier in a towel and towel-drying him well, paying special attention to his chest and underbelly. By now your Boston is all bouncy and excited and wants to go out for a walk and show off his sparkling coat. But he'll have to wait a few minutes. Keep your bundle of energy indoors until he is completely dry.

If the show ring is in your Boston's future, extra grooming touches will be necessary but he will learn to love the attention.

With a cast like this, it's no wonder that the Boston Terrier is very popular among today's dog owners.

With proper training your Boston Terrier will become a well-mannered gentleman.

TRAINING YOUR BOSTON TERRIER

You owe proper training to your Boston Terrier. The right and privilege of being trained is his birthright; and whether your Boston Terrier is going to be a handsome, well-mannered housedog and companion, a show dog, or whatever possible use he may be put to, the basic training is always the same—all must start with basic obedience, or what might be called "manner training."

Your Boston Terrier must come instantly when called and obey the "Sit" or "Down" command just as fast; he must walk quietly at "Heel," whether on or off lead. He must be mannerly and polite wherever he goes; he must be polite to strangers on the street and in stores. He must be mannerly in the presence of other dogs. He must not bark at children on roller skates,

Establish rules with your Boston—like staying down on command— so he will know what behavior is acceptable.

Condition your Boston puppy to wear a collar so he can learn how to properly walk on lead.

down his training progress. And using a "pro" trainer means that you will have to go for some training, too, after the trainer feels your Boston Terrier is ready to go home. You will have to learn how your Boston Terrier works, just what to expect of him and how to use what the dog has learned after he is home.

OBEDIENCE TRAINING CLASS

Another way to train your Boston Terrier (many experienced Boston Terrier people think this is the best) is to join an obedience training class right in your own community. There is such a group

The Nylabone/Gumabone® Pooch Pacifier enables dogs to slowly chew off the knobs while they clean their teeth. The knobs develop elastic frays which act as a toothbrush. These pacifiers are extremely effective.

motorcycles, or other domestic animals. And he must be restrained from chasing cats. It is not a dog's inalienable right to chase cats, and he must be reprimanded for it.

PROFESSIONAL TRAINING

How do you go about this training? Well, it's a very simple procedure, pretty well standardized by now. First, if you can afford the extra expense, you may send your Boston Terrier to a professional trainer, where in 30 to 60 days he will learn how to be a "good dog." If you enlist the services of a good professional trainer, follow his advice of when to come to see the dog. No, he won't forget you, but too-frequent visits at the wrong time may slow

in nearly every community nowadays. Here you will be working with a group of people who are also just starting out. You will actually be training your own dog, since all work is done under the direction of a head trainer who will make suggestions to you and also tell you when and how to correct your Boston Terrier's errors. Then, too, working with such a group, your Boston Terrier will learn to get along with other dogs. And, what

Write to your national kennel club for the location of a training club or class in your locality. Sign up. Go to it regularly—every session! Go early and leave late! Both you and your Boston Terrier will benefit tremendously.

TRAIN HIM BY THE BOOK

The third way of training your Boston Terrier is by the book. Yes, you can do it this way and do a good job of it too. But in using the book method, select a book,

Establishing control and keeping your dog's attention are two important factors in successful dog training.

is more important, he will learn to do exactly what he is told to do, no matter how much confusion there is around him or how great the temptation is to go his own way.

buy it, study it carefully; then study it some more, until the procedures are almost second nature to you. Then start your training. But stay with the book and its advice and exercises.

Your Boston Terrier's full attention is needed during training sessions.

Don't start in and then make up a few rules of your own. If you don't follow the book, you'll get into jams you can't get out of by yourself. If after a few hours of short training sessions your Boston Terrier is still not working as he should, get back to the book for a study session, because it's your fault, not the dog's! The procedures of dog training have been so well systemized that it must be your fault, since literally thousands of fine Boston Terriers have been trained by the book.

After your Boston Terrier is "letter perfect" under all conditions, then, if you wish, go on to advanced training and trick work.

Your Boston Terrier will love his obedience training, and you'll burst with pride at the finished product! Your Boston Terrier will enjoy life even more, and you'll enjoy your Boston Terrier more. And remember—you *owe good training to your Boston Terrier.*

EXERCISING YOUR BOSTON TERRIER

The smooth muscles beneath your Boston Terrier's sleek coat are not the only muscles that are toned and conditioned by regular exercise. His heart is made of muscle and even his intestine are good for both of you, but if you'd rather stay indoors, bring out your dog's toys and get him involved in a chasing, fetching or play-killing (shaking a soft toy while growling up a storm) game.

Encourage your Boston puppy to play games that both of you can enjoy. Retrieving a Gumabone® Frisbee®* is a great start. (The trademark Frisbee is used under license from Mattel, Inc. California, USA).

contains muscle tissue. Blood supply to the muscles is dependent on regular exercise. That means your Boston will live longer and be more attractive if he has sufficient exercise. He will also be better behaved. Many behavior problems in dogs can be traced to lack of exercise.

There are many ways to exercise your Boston. Brisk walks

Boston Terriers can get enough exercise in an apartment if their owners encourage them to play. Most Bostons love to chase balls and excel at learning games that can be played indoors or outdoors, such as hide and seek, keepaway, tag and tug-a-war. Just don't overdo the excitement on hot days unless the air conditioner is on.

Your young to middle-aged Boston will also be happy to exercise himself in a securely fenced yard with shade and water available, and a couple of toys. Put him out during the cooler times of day, and never leave him outside for long periods if it's warm and muggy or quite cold. When he is young, your dog will rather flimsy. When torn, they can be swallowed, dangerous squeaker and all. So, when you get your dog a squeaky toy, either watch the fun or join right in. Just keep the toy out of his reach and bring it down every few days for a few special minutes of fun.

When you aren't at home or can't take time out to watch him,

Boston Terrier puppies don't know their limits, be careful not to overdo the excitement.

help you discover games that will exercise him. Although he will still need regular exercise when he is older, you may have to initiate it.

Your Boston will surely enjoy a squeaky toy (lightweight rubber or plastic figure with a squeaker inside). However, these toys are your Boston can safely play with a chew toy made of hard nylon or the softer gummy-type nylon such as the Nylabone® or Gumabone®. Solid, hard rubber toys labeled "indestructible" are also safe and fun and will help keep your dog active and out of trouble.

Older Bostons need regular exercise too; initiate plenty of games to help keep him fit.

The eye-catching Boston often places in the Non-Sporting Group. Here Ch. El-Bo Frontier Legend takes a Group IV at the Middleburg Kennel Club show in 1988.

SHOWING YOUR BOSTON TERRIER

A show Boston Terrier is a comparatively rare thing. He is one out of several litters of puppies. He happens to be born with a degree of physical perfection that closely approximates the standard by which the breed is judged in the show ring. Such a dog should, on maturity, be able to win or approach his championship in good, fast company at the larger shows. Upon finishing his championship, he is apt to be as highly desirable as a breeding animal. As a proven stud, he will automatically command a high price for service.

Ch. Sunwoods Merrie Munchin and his handler Jerry Rigden proudly prepare for the show judge.

Showing Boston Terriers is a lot of fun—yes, but it is a highly competitive sport. While all the experts were once beginners, the odds are against a novice. You will be showing against experienced handlers, often people who have devoted a lifetime to breeding, picking the right ones, and then showing those dogs through to their championships. Moreover, the most perfect Boston Terrier ever born has faults, and in your hands the faults will be far more evident than with the experienced handler who knows how to minimize his Boston Terrier's faults. These are but a few points on the sad side of the picture.

The experienced handler, as I say, was not born knowing the ropes. He learned—*and so can you!* You can if you will put in the same time, study and keen observation that he did. But it will take time!

KEY TO SUCCESS

First, search for a truly fine show prospect. Take the puppy home, raise him by the book, and as carefully as you know how, give him every chance to mature into the Boston Terrier you hoped for. My advice is to keep your dog out of big shows, even Puppy Classes, until he is mature. Maturity in the male is roughly two years; with the female, 14 by heart. Having done this, and while your puppy is at home (where he should be) growing into a normal, healthy Boston Terrier, go to every dog show you can possibly reach. Sit at the ringside and watch Boston Terrier judging.

Ch. Scott's Stuff N Nonsense takes another Best of Breed. Her ring career was outstanding, taking over 50 Bests of Breed and more than 25 Group placements.

months or so. When your Boston Terrier is approaching maturity, start out at match shows, and, with this experience for both of you, then go gunning for the big wins at the big shows.

Next step, read the standard by which the Boston Terrier is judged. Study it until you know it

Keep your ears and eyes open. Do your own judging, holding each of those dogs against the standard, which you now know by heart.

In your evaluations, don't start looking for faults. Look for the virtues—the best qualities. How does a given Boston Terrier shape up against the standard? Having looked for and noted the virtues, then note the faults and see what prevents a given Boston Terrier from standing correctly or moving well. Weigh these faults against the virtues, since, ideally, every feature of the dog should

it? Watch carefully as the judge places the dogs in a given class. It is difficult from the ringside always to see why number one was placed over the second dog. Try to follow the judge's reasoning. Later try to talk with

Conformation to the breed standard is essential if your Boston is going to have a show career.

contribute to the harmonious whole dog.

"RINGSIDE JUDGING"

It's a good practice to make notes on each Boston Terrier, always holding the dog against the standard. In "ringside judging," forget your personal preference for this or that feature. What does the standard say about

the judge after he is finished. Ask him questions as to why he placed certain Boston Terriers and not others. Listen while the judge explains his placings, and, I'll say right here, any judge worthy of his license should be able to give reasons.

When you're not at the ringside, talk with the fanciers and breeders who have Boston

After you master the standard and your Boston approaches maturity enter as many match shows as you can before moving on to formal competition.

Terriers. Don't be afraid to ask opinions or say that you don't know. You have a lot of listening to do, and it will help you a great deal and speed up your personal progress if you are a good listener.

THE NATIONAL CLUB

You will find it worthwhile to join the national Boston Terrier club and to subscribe to its magazine. From the national club, you will learn the location of an approved regional club near you. Now, when your young Boston Terrier is eight to ten months old, find out the dates of match shows in your section of the country. These differ from regular shows only in that no championship points are given. These shows are especially designed to launch young dogs (and new handlers) on a show career.

ENTER MATCH SHOWS

With the ring deportment you have watched at big shows firmly in mind and practice, enter your Boston Terrier in as many match shows as you can. When in the ring, you have two jobs. One is to see to it that your Boston Terrier is always being seen to its best advantage. The other job is to keep your eye on the judge to see what he may want you to do next. Watch only the judge and your Boston Terrier. Be quick and be alert; do exactly as the judge directs. Don't speak to him except to answer his questions. If he does something you don't like, don't say so. And don't irritate the judge (and everybody else) by constantly talking and fussing with your dog.

In moving about the ring, remember to keep clear of dogs beside you or in front of you. It is my advice to you *not* to show your Boston Terrier in a regular point show until he is at least close to maturity and after both you and your dog have had time to perfect ring manners and poise in the match shows.

BOSTON TERRIER HEALTH

The majority of Boston Terriers are active and healthy with an average life span of 12 to 14 years.

SPECIAL CONSIDERATIONS

The Boston Terrier is one of the "brachycephalic" breeds. That means his skull is broad at the base, but short in length. While all dogs have to be protected from heatstroke, the brachycephalic breeds need special attention. Don't allow your energetic Boston to play hard during the heat of the day and avoid respiratory difficulties by keeping him out of hot, stuffy places. For example, a Boston should never be left in a closed car — not even for a minute or two.

The Boston Terrier's expressive eyes are larger and set wider apart than those of most breeds, and consequently are more prone to injury from toddlers or other pets, especially cats. Congenital eye problems in the breed include juvenile cataracts, which lead to blindness at an early age, and a lateral deviation of the eyes, commonly called cocked eyes.

Your Boston Terrier pup will be a friend and companion to you for many years. Provide him with the best care available.

The larger eyes of the Boston Terrier need careful attention. They are set wide apart and are prone to injury. They also give the breed its endearing expression.

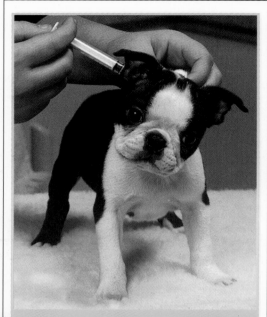

Following his puppy inoculations, your Boston will need booster vaccinations every year of his adult life.

veterinarian will set up his vaccination schedule and rid him of parasites.

VACCINATIONS ARE VITAL

Many of the most dangerous canine diseases are preventable through vaccinations, while other problems can be avoided through good nutrition and dependable daily care. Keep your puppy away from crowds of people and strange dogs until his inoculations are complete. The final puppy vaccinations are often referred to as "permanent shots," but they are only "permanent" for a year. Following his puppy series, your Boston will need booster vaccinations every year of his adult life. These vaccines protect your dog from diseases such as distemper, hepatitis, leptospirosis, parvovirus, parainfluenza,

Other genetic problems include deafness; luxated patella, a condition where the kneecap slips out of the groove (in some cases this causes no problem at all, while in other cases it cripples the dog); and heart murmurs severe enough to inhibit exercise.

To avoid buying a puppy with a problem, purchase your Boston Terrier from a reputable breeder. Choose a happy-go-lucky puppy that feels firm and full in your hands, is neither the bully nor the scaredy-cat of the litter, plays happily with his littermates and is glad to meet you. Chances are you'll have a healthy, spirited and intelligent companion for many years.

Your new Boston Terrier should visit the veterinarian for a thorough examination within 48 hours after you acquire him. The

Your Boston Terrier puppy will love to romp around outdoors. Be sure to check him for fleas and ticks after he has been outside.

tracheobronchitis, coronavirus, Lyme disease and rabies.

Distemper, an airborne virus, is the number-one killer of unvaccinated dogs and spreads rapidly from one dog to another. Occasionally a vaccinated dog also contracts the disease. Symptoms include some or all of the following: diarrhea, vomiting, reduced appetite, cough, nasal

Infectious hepatitis in dogs is not transmissible to man, although it affects the liver just as it does in the human form. Caused by canine adenovirus type I, the disease spreads through contact with an infected dog's stool, urine or saliva. Intense thirst is one indication, but other symptoms are similar to those of distemper. The disease progresses

In case of an accident, it is a good idea to keep your Boston's health and identification tags attached to its collar.

discharge, inflamed eyes, fever, exhaustion and lack of interest in toys or games. While distemper victims are usually puppies, older dogs may contract it too. Dogs that receive immediate treatment have a better chance of survival, so if you ever suspect that your Boston has distemper, take him to the veterinarian right away.

rapidly and is often fatal, so prompt veterinary treatment is critical.

Leptospirosis is caused by a microorganism that is often carried by rats. This bacteria can also be passed through the urine of an infected dog. Symptoms include bloody diarrhea and/or blood in the urine, fever,

An active and healthy breed, the Boston Terrier can have a life span of 12 to 14 years.

include loss of appetite and depression and the disease quickly progresses to diarrhea (sometimes bloody), vomiting and fever. Puppies with infected hearts (myocardial parvovirus) breathe with difficulty, may foam at the nose and mouth and often die within one or two days of contracting the disease. Those few that recover may develop chronic heart problems later. When adult Bostons contract parvovirus, reactions vary. Some become violently ill, and others just lose their appetite for a day or two before returning to normal.

From puppyhood to adulthood, your Boston's good health should be properly maintained.

depression, red and congested eyes and mouth membranes, painful mouth ulcers, vomiting, pain when moving, increased thirst, loss of appetite, and a red hue or jaundiced appearance in the whites of the eyes. Since the dog's liver and kidneys can be permanently damaged, quick veterinary treatment is essential. Humans can also contact Lepto, so observe your veterinarian's precautions if your Boston contracts this disease.

Believed to be a strain of feline distemper that mutated, the deadly **parvovirus** was unknown in dogs until 1977. The virus attacks the bone marrow, stomach lining and lymph nodes, and in young puppies, the heart. Passed through contaminated stools, it spreads rapidly from dog to dog. Early symptoms often

Parainfluenza is also known as infectious canine tracheobronchitis, and its common name is **kennel cough**. It is caused by several different viruses as well as the Bordetella bacteria, and is highly contagious from dog to dog. Symptoms of parainfluenza are a frequent dry, hacking cough and, sometimes, a nasal discharge. Adult Bostons infected with kennel cough may not even miss a meal, but the disease can be dangerous to puppies. While recovering, they should be kept in a warm, humid room. Your veterinarian may prescribe antibiotics to prevent complications and medication to control coughing for infected Bostons of all ages. Dogs vaccinated against parainfluenza sometimes come down with it anyway, but usually have milder symptoms than unvaccinated dogs.

Lyme disease is transmitted to people and dogs by two types of ticks; the more prevalent deer tick and the western black-legged tick. Symptoms of Lyme disease include fatigue, lameness, loss of appetite, fever and swollen joints. If you live in an area where the deer tick is prevalent, keep your lawn well trimmed, take precautions to keep field mice from nesting in your home and avoid walking in the woods. There is a vaccine against Lyme disease, but since Lyme was first diagnosed in dogs in 1984, the vaccine is still being perfected and isn't 100% effective yet.

Rabies is a viral disease that is always fatal, and a dog with

The Boston Terrier's large ears are a favorite place for disease-carrying ticks to hide. Always check these when grooming your Boston.

rabies is a danger to humans and other animals. A vaccine prevents this dreadful disease. Your veterinarian will give the rabies shot separately, not in combination with the other vaccines, and will tell you when your Boston's rabies vaccination should be renewed.

The rabies virus can infect dogs that come in contact with other animals, domestic or wild, that already have the virus. Rabies attacks the nervous system, and is most often spread by infected saliva — usually from a bite. It may also be transmitted through cuts or scratches that come in contact with saliva from a rabid animal.

An early sign of rabies is a change in disposition. A gentle dog may become aggressive or an aloof dog may become loving.

Plenty of fresh air and exercise will keep your Boston happy and healthy.

Later, the dog's pupils may dilate and light may become painful. Soon the dog will want to be left alone and may have stomach pains and a fever. Advanced symptoms are twitching facial muscles, bared teeth, random biting and lack of coordination. Eventually the dog loses control of his facial muscles, resulting in an open mouth with the tongue hanging out. The dog may drool, paw at his mouth and cough before he finally slips into a coma and dies. All warm-blooded animals are susceptible to rabies, so anyone bitten by a dog (or any other animal) should see a doctor right away.

CONTROLLING PARASITES

No mattter how well you take care of your Boston Terrier, he may still become infested with internal parasites such as roundworm, hookworm, whipworm and tapeworm or external parasites such as fleas, ticks and ear mites.

The symptoms of **worm infestation** usually include one or more of the following: a generally unsound appearance; a rough, dry coat; dull eyes; weight loss despite an enormous appetite; coughing; vomiting; weakness; diarrhea; and sometimes, bloody stools. Some dogs show no symptoms at all until they are seriously anemic from a heavy infestation, while others lose their appetite entirely when even mildly infested with worms. On the bright side, worms are easily controllable. Just have your veterinarian check your dog's stool at least twice a year and if medication is prescribed, give it exactly as instructed.

The hazardous **heartworm** is transmitted by mosquito bites, and 8 months or more may go by from the time a dog is bitten until the worms mature. Treatment is dangerous, but ignoring the condition is even worse. Symptoms of heartworm include weight loss, exhaustion and a chronic cough, as the worms interfere with the action of the dog's heart. The good news is that heartworm is preventable. A well-cared-for Boston won't get heartworm, because he will receive the preventative medication prescribed by his veterinarian.

Puppies should be started on a preventative program at a young age, and tested annually. Adult dogs must test free of the worms before they can begin a preventative regimen because the medication may make them deathly ill if they are already infested with adult heartworms.

Ticks, fleas and **ear mites** may all try to set up housekeeping on your Boston Terrier. Ticks come in a variety of sizes and in colors and are fairly easy to find on a Boston because of his short coat. They seem to prefer the head and neck area but may be found anywhere on the body. Your veterinarian will recommend a preparation that removes them safely and effectively. If you find a tick on your Boston when you are far away from your medicine chest, separate your dog's hair so you can see where the tick embedded itself in the skin. The embedded part is its head. Using tweezers, clamp down as close to the head as possible and pull it

Keep your Boston Terrier puppy away from crowds of people and strange dogs until his inoculations are complete.

out. If part of the head remains under your Boston's skin, apply an antiseptic.

Fleas are the most difficult parasite to get rid of. New and updated versions of flea sprays, dips and powders appear on the market every year because fleas quickly become resistant to insecticides. Your veterinarian knows which preparations work best in your locale, so if your Boston or your home is bothered by fleas, seek professional help. It's important to follow your veterinarian's instructions to the letter. Don't experiment with more than one flea remedy at the same time. A perfectly safe insecticide may become lethal to dogs when mixed with another insecticide.

Keep in close touch with your Boston so you'll know when he's not feeling up to par.

Ear mites live in the ear canal, making your Boston's sensitive ears sore and itchy, and producing a dry, rusty-brown discharge. This condition responds quickly to veterinary treatment.

CLOGGED ANAL GLANDS

If your Boston Terrier scoots along the floor on his haunches, he probably has clogged anal glands. The anal glands, located on each side of the anus, secrete a substance that helps your Boston pass his stool. They are extremely uncomfortable when clogged, smell bad and could easily become infected. Your

veterinarian can easily unclog your Boston's anal glands, or you can save yourself the trip and do it yourself. Use one hand to keep your dog's tail up and hold a soft tissue in your other hand. Take the skin on either side of the anus, just below the middle, in your thumb and forefinger. Push in slightly and squeeze gently. Soon a brownish, nasty smelling substance will stain your tissue, and your dog will stop scooting. Blood or pus in the secretion is a sign of infection, so if either one is present, take your Boston to the veterinarian.

SPAYING AND NEUTERING

The nicest thing you can do for yourself and your Boston Terrier is to have your dog spayed or neutered. Females spayed before their first season are at much less risk of developing breast cancer than unspayed females, and never develop cancers or infections of the ovaries or uterus since they have no reproductive organs. They are also easier to live with as they don't discharge all over your house for several days twice a year, or develop an urge to roam, or entice males to your door, or have unwanted, expensive and often dangerous pregnancies. Breeding a Boston Terrier is a major undertaking. Approximately ninety percent of female Bostons need a cesarean section to deliever their pups.

Neutering a male dog has its plusses too. It often makes him easier to housebreak and stablizes his disposition. Having the operation performed before he

Proper care and education can only help owners promote the health and longevity of their Boston Terriers.

is a year old could also save him the pain of prostrate problems, including cancer, when he ages.

Don't believe the old wive's tale that spaying or neutering makes a dog fat and lazy. Over feeding and lack of exercise do that. The fact is that spayed and neutered pets have better concentration and are often the top performers in obedience, agility, and other competitive sports. Spayed and neutered dogs are welcome in obedience and agility competition, but since dog shows are a showcase for breeding stock, they are not permitted to compete in conformation. If a show career is in your puppy's future, refrain from spaying or neutering until your dog retires from competition.

SUGGESTED READING

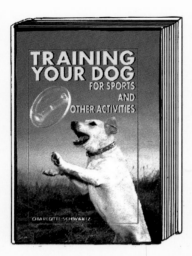

**TRAINING YOUR DOG FOR
SPORTS AND OTHER ACTIVITIES**
by Charlotte Schwartz
TS-258

**THE ATLAS OF DOG BREEDS
OF THE WORLD**
by Bonnie Wilcox, DVM, and Chris Walkowicz
H-1091

SUCCESSFUL DOG TRAINING
by Michael Kramer
TS-205

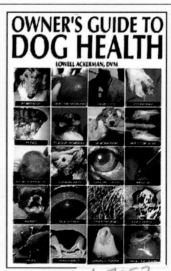

**OWNER'S GUIDE TO
DOG HEALTH**
by Lowell Ackerman, DVM
TS-214